Start Your Engines

Riding Dirt Bikes

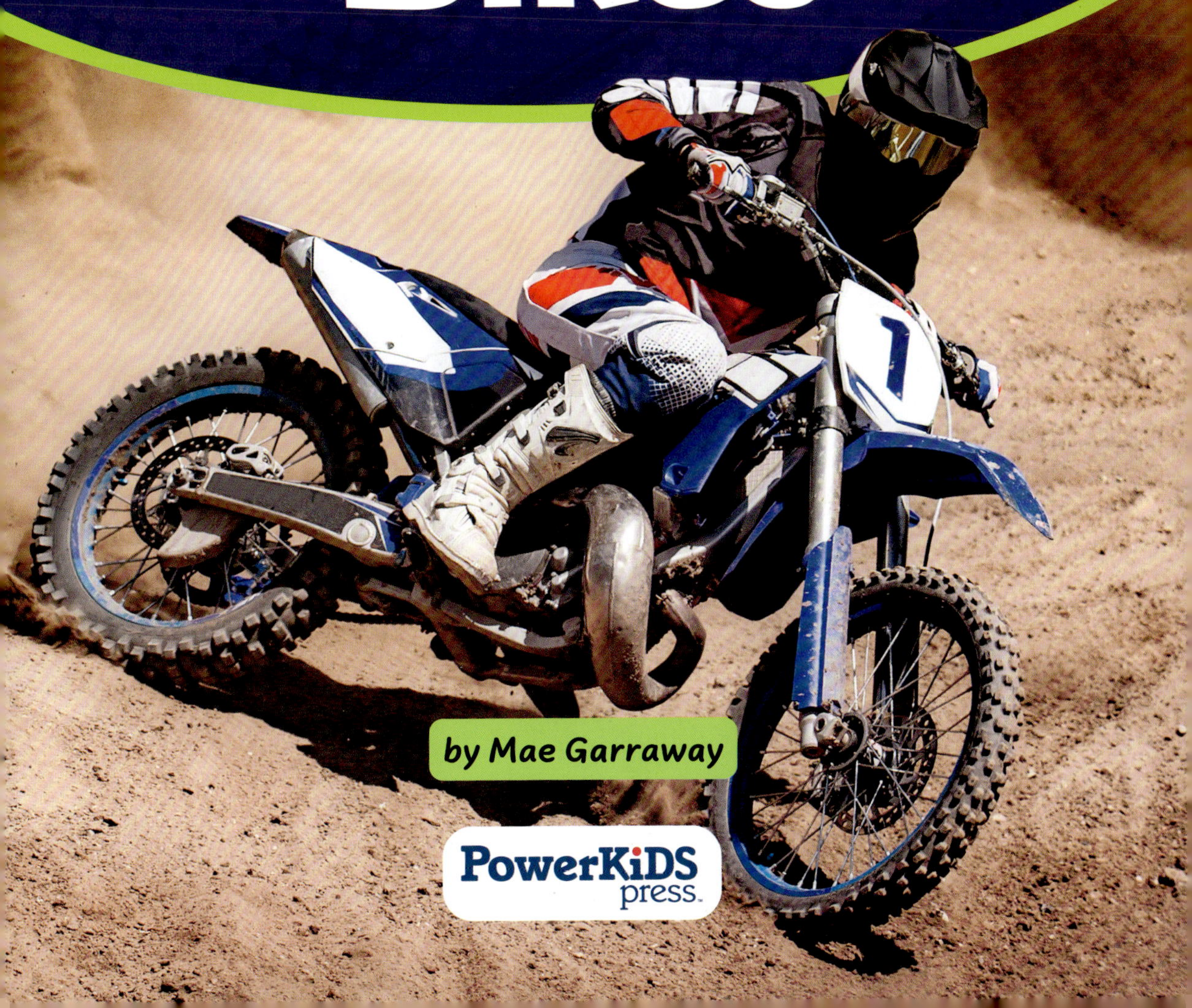

by Mae Garraway

PowerKiDS press.

Published in 2027 by The Rosen Publishing Group, Inc.
2544 Clinton Street, Buffalo, NY 14224

Portions of this work were originally authored by Wendy Hinote Lanier and published as *Dirt Bikes*. All new material in this edition was authored by Mae Garraway.

Editor: Claire Vanden Branden
Book Design: Joshua Olson

Photo Credits: Cover, pp. 1, 9 Maciej Kopaniecki/Shutterstock.com; p. 4 Dave Hewison Photography/Shutterstock.com; p. 7 Luti/Shutterstock.com; p. 10 Library of Congress; p. 13 Edu_2ev/Shutterstock.com; pp. 15, 18, 29 Sonrak/Shutterstock.com; p. 16 sainthorant/Shutterstock.com; p. 20 Felix Mizioznikov/Shutterstock.com; p. 22 Maxim Petrichuk/Shutterstock.com; p. 25 J. A. Dunbar/Shutterstock.com; p. 27 nattanan726/Shutterstock.com.

Cataloging-in-Publication Data
Names: Garraway, Mae.
Title: Riding dirt bikes / Mae Garraway.
Description: Buffalo, New York : PowerKids Press, 2027. | Series: Start your engines | Includes glossary and index.
Identifiers: ISBN 9781538296264 (pbk.) | ISBN 9781538296271 (library bound) | ISBN 9781538296288 (ebook)
Subjects: LCSH: Motocross--Juvenile literature. | Trail bikes--Juvenile literature.
Classification: LCC GV1060.12 G377 2027 | DDC 796.756--dc23

Printed in China

CPSIA Compliance Information: Batch #QS27PK. For Further Information contact Rosen Publishing, at 1-800-237-9932.

TABLE OF CONTENTS

CLUBMX
ATVS&MORE
DUNLOP
YAMALUBE
MUC-OFF
GYTR
FIREPOWER
OGIO
FXR
16

Chapter 1

Dirt Bike Races

It's race day at the Daytona Supercross in Daytona Beach, Florida. The stands are full for the 250 event. Thousands of fans have gathered to watch. The riders ease into the starting gate.

There are dirt bikes that can reach up to 120 miles per hour (193 km/h).

The gate drops, and the riders surge forward. Rider number 6 reaches the first turn ahead of the pack and claims the **holeshot**. He's in the lead. On the next curve, he **brake checks** the rider behind him in an effort to slow him down. The riders go over **whoop-de-dos** and around tight turns.

Fun Fact

Arenacross is an indoor version of motocross that uses smaller courses.

Some dirt bike races can have up to 30 racers.

With only one lap to go, the rider in the lead leans too far to the left. He wipes out. Number 24 flies past. The new leader skids around the next curve. He sends up a **rooster tail** of dirt behind him.

The crowd roars as he takes the checkered flag.

The Daytona Supercross is part of a racing series called the Monster Energy AMA Supercross Championship. The series is a set of races. They take place across the United States. Riders are given points based on what place they finish in each race. The rider with the most points at the end of the series is named the champion. Top riders can win thousands of dollars.

A rooster tail can make visibility difficult for other riders.

Indian

Chapter 2

History of Dirt Bikes

Motorcycles were first introduced in the late 1800s. At first, they were simply motorized bicycles. But by the early 1900s, companies were building motorcycles very similar to today's.

These motorcycles from the early 1900s are not much different from modern motorcycles.

Companies began organizing races to test their latest models and interest buyers. Soon, motorcycle companies were building racing courses and bikes to race on them.

One of the first competitions was an enduro race. This off-road race was created to test riders' **endurance**. The first enduro competition took place in 1913. Others followed. Each race lasted many hours. Some lasted days. Riders followed a path over different

Motocross jumps often send riders high into the air.

types of ground surfaces. The goal was to maintain a certain speed throughout the race.

Races evolved. By the mid-1920s, outdoor courses were made featuring jumps and tight turns.

Originally called scrambles, these races tested a rider's ability to go over natural and man-made **obstacles**. By the mid-1900s, this type of race was known as motocross.

Fun Fact

The American Motorcyclist Association (AMA) establishes racing rules for all types of motorcycle events. AMA racing series include supercross, motocross, endurocross, and dirt track.

Each race has a set number of laps that a driver must complete.

In the 1970s, a new type of racing called supercross brought motocross into arenas and stadiums. These courses included high jumps, closely spaced bumps, and many turns.

Chapter 3

All About Dirt Bikes

Dirt bikes are off-road motorcycles. They are much lighter and easier to handle than road bikes. Most dirt bikes do not have windshields, lights, or turn signals. This kind of bike is not legal to drive on the street.

A dirt bike race starts out with a large pack of riders trying to get the best position.

Jumps often have large ruts that can make it difficult to control the bike.

Engine sizes range from 50 cubic centimeters (cc) to more than 500cc. The engines are usually two-stroke or four-stroke. Two-stroke engines are lighter. They work well on loose, sandy dirt.

Four-stroke engines are heavier. They provide greater control in ruts and on hard-packed dirt.

Dirt bikes have a special **suspension** system for a smoother ride. Their large, knobby tires give the bikes traction on all kinds of surfaces.

Fun Fact

Dirt bike goggles have layers of plastic sheets on them. During a race, a rider can tear off each layer when it gets too dirty to see through.

Some riders can do backflips midair.

It's important for riders to stay safe when they race. They wear full-body suits that are made of leather. The suits have padding by the shoulders, elbows, knees, and hips. This padding helps protect riders' bodies if they fall. Riders also wear helmets, gloves, and boots. However, dirt biking is risky. Even with safety gear, riders may get injured.

Supercells form when spinning wind moves upward through clouds.

Rain pours down. Dark clouds rise high into the sky. Air inside some clouds starts to spin. The storm chasers drive toward them.

Chapter 4

Dirt Bikes Today

Dirt bike racing is a thrilling **professional** sport. But people also ride dirt bikes just for fun, including kids. To stay safe, they can start on flat, open ground. And they should always wear safety gear.

Riders sometimes put their feet down for balance.

Today's dirt bikes enable skilled riders to do outrageous moves. Advanced suspension systems, disc brakes, and better four-stroke engines have made this possible.

Common dirt bike makers include Honda, Yamaha, Kawasaki, and Suzuki. These companies produce

Fun Fact

Electric dirt bikes are gaining popularity in motorbike racing. These bikes use motors and batteries instead of gas-powered engines.

Children as young as four years old could start riding dirt bikes as a hobby.

bikes with various engine sizes and a variety of frames. Some are designed for professional racing. Others are strictly recreational bikes that make off-roading fun for everyone.

Dig Deeper!

Dirt Bike Suspension

Dirt bikes have two suspension systems. The front suspension is made of a fork attached to the front wheel. Each side of the fork has springs that move up and down as the bike goes over bumps. Inside the spring is a fluid-filled strut that helps cushion the impact.

The rear suspension is a spring and strut combination attached to the bike's frame and rear wheel. These systems help the rider maintain control and increase speed.

Suspension systems help riders handle their bikes on bumpy tracks.

Test Your KNOWLEDGE

Take this quiz to test your knowledge.

1. Write a sentence that summarizes the main idea of Chapter 4.
2. Do you think children should be allowed to ride dirt bikes? Why or why not?
3. When did supercross first appear?
   - A. the late 1800s
   - B. the early 1900s
   - C. the 1970s
4. Why don't riders use regular motorcycles in motocross races?
   - A. because regular motorcycles are too slow
   - B. because regular motorcycles are too heavy
   - C. because regular motorcycles are too expensive

5. What does **traction** mean in this book?

*Dirt bikes have a special suspension system for a smoother ride. Their large, knobby tires give the bikes **traction** on all kinds of surfaces.*

A. bump
B. grip
C. dirt

6. What does **recreational** mean in this book?

*Some are designed for professional racing. Others are strictly **recreational** bikes that make off-roading fun for everyone.*

A. done for a long time
B. done for money
C. done for fun

Answers can be found on page 32.

GLOSSARY

brake checks
When a rider slows down quickly, causing the rider behind him or her to do the same.

endurance
The ability to continue riding in spite of strain, pain, or difficulty.

holeshot
When a rider is the first one to reach the first corner of a race.

obstacles
Things that get in the way.

professional
Done as a way to earn money.

rooster tail
A spray of dirt behind a motorcycle.

suspension
A system of shock absorbers and springs that help maintain a smooth ride.

whoop-de-dos
Large bumps on a dirt bike trail, also called whoops.

FOR MORE INFORMATION

BOOKS

Amstutz, Lisa J. *Motocross: Turns and Berms*. Mankato, MN: Capstone Press, 2026.

Golusky, Jackie. *Supercross: Rev It Up!* Minneapolis, MN: Lerner Publications, 2023.

WEBSITES

American Motorcyclist Association
americanmotorcyclist.com/racing/motocross/
Learn more about the different motocross races at this website.

Britannica Kids: Motorcycle Racing
kids.britannica.com/students/article/motorcycle/275952
Learn more about the history of motorcycles and motocross racing.

Publisher's note to educators and parents: Our editors have carefully reviewed these websites to ensure that they are suitable for students. Many websites change frequently, however, and we cannot guarantee that a site's future contents will continue to meet our high standards of quality and educational value. Be advised that students should be closely supervised whenever they access the internet.

INDEX

Answer Key: 1. Answers will vary; 2. Answers will vary; 3. C; 4. B; 5. B; 6. C